MEN ONLY

MEN ONLY:
Relationship Advice From Men to
Help Women Choose Better, Avoid Heartbreak
& Stop Wasting Time

Published by Krystle Laughter LLC
Tacoma, WA 98409

Printed in the United States of America

Cover & Interior Design by Krystle Laughter
ISBN 978-1-955787-29-1

MEN ONLY

Relationship Advice From Men to Help Women Choose Better

KRYSTLE LAUGHTER

TABLE OF CONTENTS

DISCLAIMER

Some comments have been slightly changed or altered to help with readability and comprehension.

Thank You!!

To all of the men who provided wisdom, honesty, and insight to women in need. May God Richly Bless You.

**This book was inspired by a viral post by @wildseedwildflower

The original question was asked by @itsnwts

I have done my best to acknowledge the people who have contributed to this book. Thank you for the inspiration.

INTRODUCTION

This book was inspired by a social media discussion from a woman asking men for dating advice. As I read the post, I realized that many women lack a basic understanding of men, their behaviors, and how they think; which often leads to confusion, wasted time, and heartbreak. At the request of the women on that post, I decided to compile all the dating advice from the men, as well as some of my own insights, to help women move from surviving to thriving in their dating lives. This book should be used as a guide to help you navigate the often challenging world of men.

My goal is to help women by educating, informing, and encouraging them not to lose hope. You can learn to detach and avoid unserious men and make time for the men who deserve your time.

Ladies, you have so much to give, and I want you to give it to the right man. I want you to know your worth. You're not asking too much. You're just asking the wrong person. It may hurt now, but in the end, you'll be better off. You are smart, beautiful, and capable of choosing the right partner for your life and needs. Trust yourself!

"If you don't learn how to love yourself first, someone will offer you less than you deserve, and you'll accept it".

–Love Yourself First

MEN ONLY:

Dating & Relationship Advice

Advice from @eyedealblackman

Women, let me save you 2 years of your life. If he likes you, you will not be confused. Confusion is not chemistry. Anxiety is not butterflies. Inconsistency is not "he's busy." Stop dating potential. Start dating patterns.

You are not Build-A-Man University. If he:

- disappears when things get hard
- only calls when it benefits him
- avoids defining the relationship
- makes you compete for his attention

That is not a mystery. That is immaturity. A man ready for you will:

- move with consistency
- protect your peace
- communicate clearly
- make you feel secure, not anxious

Additionally, if you feel like you're auditioning, he's not casting you, and let's be honest. Some of y'all aren't in love. You're attached to the attention. High-value women don't chase validation. They choose alignment.

Ask Yourself This:

Would I want my daughter dating a man like this? If the answer is no, stop romanticizing him. Never beg a man to choose you. The right one won't need convincing. Love should feel like growth. Not survival.

Notes to Self:

Advice from @treyyoungda1

He thought about you before he did it, and still did.

Advice from @instakino

You don't have to sleep with a man you're dating to show him you're into him. If he pays for 2 dates, you should offer to pay for the 3rd. He most likely won't let you pay, but he'll know you're not there just for the free food and the experience. If he gives you $100, take $20 out of that $100 he gave you and buy him something with it.

It can be as simple as a tank top. It's the gesture that counts. Basic reciprocity shows a man that the relationship is not one-sided. You don't have to sleep with him. MOST WOMEN WERE NEVER TAUGHT HOW TO KEEP A MAN WITHOUT HAVING TO SLEEP WITH HIM. If he's doing nice things for you, reciprocate.

Advice from @thederekoscar

Men aren't complicated. If he's treating you like you don't matter, it's because you don't matter to him. Don't play yourself trying to overthink and defend his behavior.

Advice from @yojd1

There is no fixing him. Move on.

Advice from @g_rant_36

Trust your instincts about him. You're probably right.

Reflection Notes:

Advice from @itskriscope

Forgiveness can happen without reconnection. Some lessons are learned from a distance.

Advice from @therootedholistics

Pay attention to a man's actions more than his words. Words mean nothing without action.

Advice from @samsimonvil

Learn to walk away, or accept the man you chose, instead of trying to change him into another man.

Advice from @mrjaywrkin

The man with $100 to his name who gave you $60 loves you way more than the guy with 100k who took you to Miami and got you a bag. (This Comment isn't about Money)

Advice from @therootedholistics

Unpopular opinion - not every man is a leader.

Advice from @enriquelondon28

If he does it once, he'll do it again.

Advice from @jusstephen

Let a man lead where he's strong, but watch if he's willing to grow where he's weak.

Advice from @christen_em

Children make mistakes. Adults make choices.

Advice from @cole.thefirst

When he shows you who he is, believe him the first time. Don't make excuses.

Advice from @___.mopsy.___

When a man truly cares, his efforts are never transactional. He doesn't love expecting something in return. He simply wants to be with her. Sometimes, all he desires is to look into her eyes and get lost there.

Her smile becomes his smile. Her tears become his concern. He wipes them away and tries to bring her joy again.

He listens, he understands, and most importantly, he accepts her exactly as she is.... If you find someone like this... never lose them.

Advice from @justcallmetone

He's ALWAYS thinking about way more than you think he is. When we're silent, we're worried about taking care of you, making you happy, making sure our kids are good, and then last comes our survival.

Advice from @outtatown_rell4
You don't gotta beg or force a man to do nothing. If he likes you, he'll do it naturally. Stop forcing what's not meant to be.

Advice from @eyedealblackman
Learn to be alone before you try to build with someone. Loneliness will make you tolerate things you normally would not.

Advice from @hm_majesty
Be vocal if you don't like something; say it. If we don't listen, say it again until we do. Plus, ladies, when you get into a relationship, don't forget about you. We never forget about ourselves, be self-aware, and look after number one sometimes.

Advice from @azuka_ezefili
If I could give relationship advice to women, the first and most priceless thing would be this: Love yourself before you attempt to love someone else. A man can only love you and appreciate you for exactly who you see yourself as, so if you lack self-worth and boundaries, he will treat you as such and push you to the brink. The more you stand tall in your love for yourself, the easier it'll be to decipher those who move with intention and purpose about YOU!

Reflection Notes:

Advice from @yungnicmusic
If a man confides in you, NEVER BRING UP WHAT HE TOLD YOU DURING AN ARGUMENT! He will never trust you again.

Advice from @rekedaddy
Don't tell him how he feels?

Advice from @rlamb_chops
You are a reflection of who you deal with!

Advice from @yozay_1115
He knows if he wants to marry you before you even start to question if he wants to marry you.

Advice from @themalcolmaskew
Giving men a second chance is disrespectful to yourself. If you truly value your self-worth as a woman, it should never happen.

Advice from @iam_thatguy_fatie
If you've rejected him before or made him wait for a long time, never, I repeat, never accept him; you will regret it.

Reflection Notes:

Men Only: Dating & Relationship Advice

Advice from @mrkeepthapartygoin
Don't love him for his potential or what you imagine that he could be. Ask yourself this question: If that man never changes, will you love him forever?

Advice from @jnealthegreatig
Pick a man you'll listen to, someone whose direction you'll trust & move forward without a doubt.

Advice from @itscliffyinsta
If a man invites you over to his house on the first date, steal something before you leave so he can understand stranger danger.

Advice from @ricky_havok
1.) Talk less. Listen more. Ask questions for clarity and stop hanging on to assumptions. Let him finish his sentences.

2.) Many women were taught growing up what to expect from a man and how a man should treat them. They were not taught how to actually treat a man. Sit with yourself and figure out if you've actually learned that skill, and if not...start learning it.

3.) Control your sense of pride. You don't know everything, and you aren't always right. None of us are.

4.) Learn to control your emotions and aim to become emotionally balanced, mature, and intelligent.

5.) Comparison is the thief of joy. What works for your friends and their relationship may not work for you and yours.

6.) You will have to grow and change. The concept of simply "accept me for me" is a flawed one, and is essentially asking a man to accept your mediocrity when we know that you're capable of more and better.

Reflection Notes:

Advice from @bizzyboybullies

A gem I got recently is that your intent doesn't always outweigh the impact of your actions or words.

Listen to your man's feelings without being defensive. Nothing says you care more than good communication and being accountable enough to say you're sorry.

Live healthy to keep both of you looking good. Keep that man fed. Nothing is sexier than bae bringing a plate of something good.

Value your man's opinion, modern women feel like almost every suggestion is an attempt to control them when your man is just telling you what he likes. Compliance doesn't equal control; it's compromise and giving parts of yourself to the person you say you want to spend your entire life with, which should also be reciprocated!!!!

Give your man the goods when he wants them, don't make him beg for them. This'll keep real ones from straying!

Reflection Notes:

Advice from @yellowyellow197y
Just because he keeps coming back to you doesn't mean he's obsessed with you. It means you're easy & convenient. That's it!

Advice from @curtfloatn
Stop moving like it's always about what you can get. The right mindset is: How can we build? What can I bring to the table? When a man feels valued, he moves differently and will naturally want to give you the world.

Advice from @nustynusta
Stop ruining your friendships because you have a new man. I've seen this way too many times. The chances of a good friendship lasting a lifetime are way higher than this relationship. If you were supposed to have a get-together with your homegirl today, go, have fun. Stop losing relationships that existed before this man got there.

Advice from @_krd_yin_
Put God first! Accept yourself before you give yourself. Build confidence outside of the visual prowess of society. Be a strong, independent THINKER, or you'll absorb other women and their bad choices.

We are all in development, stop internalizing everything like life is happening to you and not for you! You are not born perfect & exempt from the Lord's building process!

Master your emotions, study scripture for the best transformation of who you are on the inside! Do not just highlight scripture that makes you seem perfect and exempt from the inner work! We see a lot of Proverb 31 - Yet the book Proverbs is full of warnings and of what not to be. I put this last so it can be the last thing on your mind!

**These are things I put in my notes for my daughter.

Advice from @k.tiller_

Date men who actually show up for you and stop ignoring red flags!

Advice from @johnyeahthatjohn

If he's making an effort, give him a chance or two, but no more; if he's not, don't.

Advice from @malonetoole

If he's consistently being inconsistent, then he's never going to change. That's on you if you keep giving him chances and expect differently.

Advice from @melcurrantly

Everyone makes mistakes, but a pattern is not a mistake. Sometimes it's a blindness, sometimes a carelessness, sometimes a cruelty. Make boundaries, but remember that not every slight is intentional, and sometimes there is hope. BUT THERE SHOULD ALWAYS BE CONSEQUENCES (Sorry, I don't usually yell, but this one felt warranted).

Advice from @senecaorris

I saw a video of a guy saying, "You think I want you back cause I love you, but the truth is that I want you back cause you're easy. You let me treat you so much poorer than other women cause you've convinced yourself I've changed, and maybe I'll be just a little better for a while once we're back together. Long enough to pull you back. Just good enough to make you think there's hope. I'll always go back to who I was, though. I know you'll just keep letting me treat you badly, and you'll always take me back. I just need to be a little better for a little while to keep you hopeful. The truth is, I am capable of change, of treating you exactly how you should be treated. I won't because you're not important enough to me. You're my placeholder until I find someone I think is worth it, and you're not cause you allow me to be this way."

Advice from @altruism_and_adventure

Be feminine, kind, nurturing, loyal, honest, gentle, soft, and ladylike. Be a woman and let the man be a man. Don't be loud, aggressive, demanding, argumentative, dramatic, chaotic, emotional, mean, entitled, selfish, greedy, shallow, superficial, emasculating. If you want to get treated well, don't say it. Just be the person and do the things that deserve that treatment.

Advice from @s.un.lo

Respect one another's boundaries. Don't get too comfortable in conversation or action. He has feelings just like you do. Respect means more than your words, and it's shown in action, especially around others. If you can't see it as just you and him versus everyone else, don't waste his time. If he doesn't have a spiritual life, then he's not concerned about yours either. Initiate contact; it shows continued interest. Lastly, if you give him $5, he will give you $50; the thought counts and goes a very long way.

Advice from @kieranj.m

A man will love you how he likes to be loved; it won't always be how you think love is shown. Don't expect him to be something, then be disappointed he's not how you imagined.

Advice from @philthereal__

Learn to appreciate a man being all about you, and stop taking advantage of a man who wants to build a life with you. Most women want a man who is already established, looking to have a good life without seeing the beauty of growth with one another.

Advice from @stevecauthren

There are mistakes, and there are patterns. One might call for repair, the other does not. Deciding preemptively that you'll never give second chances doesn't create sustainable relationships.

Advice from @fortune.darnell

Oh, and men don't care how much you make; we want women fit, feminine, friendly, and cooperative. If you can't do that and you make 99k plus, it'll be hard for you to get married.

Advice from @kelvin1147_

Always talk things out! If there's an effort support him.

Advice from @trcsoul

Don't think in absolutes. Teach YOUR man your emotions and learn his logic. Seduce your man. You're an experience for the rest of his life. Choose you both instead of yourself (It'll teach him that you value the union, and he will protect it). Respect him, with your words, your thoughts, your everything, because he never forgets when the person closest to him hurts him.

Reflection Notes:

Men Only: Dating & Relationship Advice

Advice from @ryyglizz
Learn not to be played with the first time. If you see bad signs, RUN!

Advice from @eazi_blvk
You don't teach a man to treat you right; he studies you, and he surely knows what you want.

Advice from @brooklynewy
Don't get comfortable after you get him, and act like your work is done. A good relationship requires maintenance.

Advice from @bigwesternpromises
Unless you're dealing with a super extrovert, most men don't have the time or patience to talk all day. Most of us are comfortable with solitude and with it being just peace and quiet to ourselves.

Advice from @brooklynewy
Men can't read your mind. Communicate your feelings and give him a chance to adjust.

Advice from @enzokuhle5889
Learn to normalize saying a problem in a relationship and walking away nicely, rather than just going behind someone's back and cheating.

Reflection Notes:

Dating Advice From a Certified Life Coach

The best dating/relationship advice I've learned has been from my own lived experience. If I could give you my best advice in one minute, it'd be this: Love yourself before trying to love anyone else. When you lack the fundamental understanding of your own wants, needs, expectations, and desires, it will be nearly impossible for someone else to give you what you aren't even aware you need.

When you love out of ignorance of your own needs, you end up choosing people who are out of alignment with who you are and where you're going. That person may fit your life momentarily, but can they grow with you where you're going? Will they help you or hold you back?

Will they be able to cheer you on or discourage you from success due to their own insecurities?

When you don't know who you are, you don't know who you need. You need to make it your job to know yourself, learn yourself, and give yourself the love that you desire from others. Once you master and fall in love with yourself, you'll be able to easily recognize when others don't love you, because you will have already learned to love and value yourself. ***Real recognizes real!***

Advice from @uzicking

If you aren't a baddie without surgery, don't expect the sun, the moon & stars. Go to the gym, eat healthy, drink water & be nice.

Advice from @bestman_thethird

After the man you meet meets all that superficial stuff on the first page, find out if he's stupid, evil, or disgusting. And don't try to rationalize it if he is one of these things, because it'll be you who looks like Boo Boo The Fool.

Advice from @smitty_ditr

Listen to understand, not respond, and make sure you have clarity of what he actually said before responding. Don't respond based on your perception of what you thought you heard or read.

Advice from @btw_alec

Don't punish him for not knowing who you are, your likes, dislikes, turn-ons, turn-offs, boundaries, etc. Without properly communicating. Also, continue to communicate throughout the relationship if your needs/wants change. The worst thing you can do is just to expect him to "just know" without any prior communication. Also, don't be afraid to be direct when you communicate.

You can be soft and direct. Be patient with mistakes unless it's obvious disrespect. Most of the time, what someone likes or dislikes in a relationship might not apply to you, but he may have thought, "well my past partner responded positively/negatively to this behavior", so this person most likely will do the same. Grace will carry you far.

Advice from @blackbillionaire2027
Be vulnerable with him, let him know how you truly feel. Open communication can heal a lot of things from both sides. Remember, keep God at the center of your relationships.

Reflection Notes:

A Love Letter to Myself:

Advice from @sincerenoblemason

Learn to be your fullest, most complete self mentally, spiritually, physically, and financially. Cultivate self-love, and you can thereby navigate relationships of all kinds. Some you'll learn from. Some you'll teach. Some you'll hold onto. Some you'll release. I feel this advice could be applicable regardless of gender.

Advice from @bakedbeansots

I think most men are pretty similar in simplicity, so I'll try to give the most universal advice. I think the biggest problem women face is retaining the men that they encounter or making the men they encounter want to see them in a long-term sense.

A lot of that comes down to not understanding or considering what a man may need or want in order for him to show up the way that a man should.

At a very baseline men are pretty simple in wanting an easygoing connection. "Peace" is what most would call it. It's not being a doormat or cooking and cleaning. It's the commitment to wanting to make a man's life easier than it currently is. Showing up in a way that welcomes him to feel like he's also emotionally protected. Get to know the man and have a genuine interest in who he is, what he likes, and what's important to him.

Essentially, be his "peace/escape" in a world that already doesn't acknowledge his importance. If you do that, that man isn't going anywhere.

Advice from @your.pal.dirte
Respectfully... know when to just let him lead. He's capable.

Advice from @majorcustoms704
Always consider what you wouldn't want someone to do to you before you do it to them.

Advice from @true_hyde
Stop listening to other bitter women online because they will negatively influence you on how to deal with men. Learn to be feminine, not CONDITIONALLY feminine. Be modest. Cook good meals. Keep your hygiene on point.

Advice from @uade__876
Try to add value to his life in any form of way.

Advice from @1stkingofzamunda
If you're gonna end things with a man, always tell him the real reason. Don't give cop out answers that don't actually ring true.

WHAT I WANT IN A MAN:

Think in terms of character, not looks or income. What type of person is your dream man? Is he patient, kind, safe, flexible, loyal? Spontaneous? Think along those lines.

WHAT I NEED IN A MAN:

Consider your past and present dating history, your life experiences, your personality, your trauma, pet peeves, physical and emotional needs, and shortcomings. Write down what you need in a partner, based on a man who will be considerate, compassionate, and best tailored to you. Remember, you need someone who will fit into the intricacies of your life now and as you grow.

MY DEAL BREAKERS

This is where you list the behaviors and actions you will not tolerate from a man in a relationship. Again, this is based on knowing thyself, your wants, and your needs. For example, I will not tolerate a man who has kids under one year of age. I will not date a man with a known history of violence against women. I will not date a man who doesn't provide for his children, etc...

10 DATING AFFIRMATIONS

1. I will love myself first.
2. I will treat myself the way I want a man to treat me.
3. I will love myself the way I want a man to love me.
4. I am worthy of the love I desire, and I will have it.
5. I am beautiful, successful, and confident.
6. I will not chase men. I attract them.
7. I am not waiting to be chosen. I do the choosing.
8. I will not entertain confusion. If there's confusion, I'm losing.
9. I will not let men waste my time. I have options.
10. My worth isn't based on my relationship status.

Reflection Notes:

MY DATING AFFIRMATIONS

MY DATING AFFIRMATIONS

ABOUT THE AUTHOR

Krystle Laughter is an international best-selling author, certified life coach, mentor, and creator of Krystle Laughter Academy, an online school to help women heal and build self-confidence. She also helps people create, market, and self-publish their books.

She is the author of the best-selling series: Love Yourself First, He Doesn't Love You If..., and Let's Be Honest: Real Answers for Real Women Facing Abuse. In her spare time, she enjoys mentoring women on her YouTube channel, gardening, watching period dramas, and spending time with her children.

Visit **krystlelaughteracademy.com** to start your healing and self-publishing journey!

MY STORY

I've made a lot of mistakes when it comes to men and dating. In 2019, I was pregnant, separated, and going through a divorce from my then-husband. Years of toxic and gaslighting behaviors had taken their toll on me, and I finally got the courage to ask him to leave. I held on so long because I didn't want to be a single mother. I finally decided that it was better to be a single mom of multiple children than to subject myself to neglect, instability and abuse for the rest of my life.

At this time, I enrolled in counseling and decided to improve myself by deeply reflecting on my past relationships and discovering how I had gotten into this mess. Through self-reflection, honesty, and therapy, I was able to get to the root cause of my settling and abusive relationships and learn how to love myself for the first time in my life.

I put all of my experience and lessons into ***the Love Yourself First Series available on Amazon.***
Since then, I have gone on to write numerous self-help books, children's books, create online courses, and make YouTube videos to help women all over the world heal and move forward in life in relationships. Thank you for letting me share my story with you.

-Sincerely,
Krystle Laughter

BOOKS BY THE AUTHOR

The Love Yourself First Series

Love Yourself First

Love Yourself Again

Love Yourself First: Kids teaches children of all ages the basics of self-love in a simplified way

LYF: The Workbook

LYF: Affirmation Journal

GET ALL BOOKS ON:

amazon

Krystle Laughter Academy

Love Yourself First: Next Steps

Online Course

Love Yourself First.

NEXT STEPS

- Learn to be Confident
- Heal from the Inside Out
- Rebuild Your Self-Esteem
- Develop Standards for Life

Get the knowledge and skills needed to be self-confident in relationships, heal from past toxic relationships, rebuild broken self-esteem & create healthy standards for your life and relationships.

Find this course and many more at

KrystleLaughterAcademy.com

He Doesn't Love You If...

Stop wondering if he's really into you and learn the 10 telltale signs that a man is wasting your time.

Reflection Notes:

www.ingramcontent.com/pod-product-compliance
Lightning Source LLC
LaVergne TN
LVHW011051110826
845149LV00015B/3455

* 9 7 8 1 9 5 5 7 8 7 2 9 1 *

Develop Your Author Voice

Strengthen Your Writing Style and Create a Voice Readers Recognize

The *Write Boost* Writing Series

Karina Fabian

Laser Cow Press

MERRITT ISLAND, FL

Laser Cow Press
Merritt Island, FL
https://fabianspace.com

Book Layout © 2017 BookDesignTemplates.com
Cover art by Karina Fabian using Canva AI

Developing Your Author Voice/ Karina Fabian -- 1st ed.
ISBN 978-1-956489-28-6